"Inner Whispers"

Messages From A Spirit Guide

April Crawford

"Inner Whispers": Messages From A Spirit Guide...

Author: April Crawford

Publisher: Connecting Wave
2629 Foothill Blvd.
Unit # 353
La Crescenta, CA 91214
www.ConnectingWave.com

ISBN: 978-0-9823269-1-6

For Author Information: www.AprilCrawford.com

Other books via April Crawford:
www.AprilCrawfordBookStore.com

Book Design: Allen Crawford

Cover Photo: Toni Sipka

For Permissions: Publisher@ConnectingWave.com

CONTENTS

About April Crawford

April Crawford is a natural Open Deep Trance Channel and Spirit Medium. These are relatively rare.

Because April is able to be completely open and without any fear of the process whatsoever, the nonphysical entities and guides who come through are able to <u>totally</u> integrate with the physical, while at the same time not blending at all with April's personality. They therefore have <u>full</u> physical and emotional, control during their "visits".

This allows zero distortion or "coloring" by April, and also allows them to walk around the room, go out for a walk in the night air, keep their eyes wide open when they speak, and even eat or drink if they wish (but most choose not to).

These physical abilities are one of the things that allow VERONICA... the name we have given to the highly evolved nonphysical entity and guide that gave us most of the messages in this book... to give readings and have long fully interactive conversations over a speakerphone, and even to write in longhand herself (not automatic writing), or type on a computer keyboard and even use a computer mouse or computer touch screen.

You can see videos of VERONICA speaking while April Crawford is in deep trance at:

www.AprilCrawford.com

April routinely allows many different entities and aspects of entities to come through, and they have a full range of motion and emotion. Some who are in-between physical lives, for example, have cried uncontrollably or expressed total joy when we advised them of certain things about their physical lives.

About VERONICA

The Spirit Guide that wrote most of these messages is VERONICA. There are a few others that have added some messages also, and they are noted.

"VERONICA", as we call "her", is an evolved nonphysical entity and guide. "She" refers to herself as a nonphysical consciousness and she leans toward female energy even though VERONICA has been both sexes and she has told me her favorite physical life was as a male.

(Note: Some other entities and individuals in-between physical lives that come through April Crawford express

themselves as male energies, so it is not because April is female that VERONICA expresses herself as female.)

You may wonder about VERONICA's name. Actually, it is a name we gave her many years ago. When she first came through, it was rather amazing and rather dramatic (and VERONIA was not the first to come through, but was certainly the most intense). At that time, "she" did not give us a name when we asked, saying basically that "Labels are not necessary". She went on to say that if we needed a label, that we could choose whatever name we wanted.

We chose "VERONICA", and it stuck. Now, even other nonphysical beings who visit via April Crawford's Open Deep Trance Channeling know exactly who VERONICA is. It seems that things get around in the cosmos rather quickly and rather completely!

All of VERONICA's messages are either spoken or written by her in first, final, and only draft. There is never any editing of a single sentence or word.

1

The Rhythm of Your Soul

"How often in your daily life do you sense a pulse of energy? An underlying communication that ever flows but in some instances eludes embracement? The rhythm of your soul continually attempts to align itself with your reality... subtle enough for impact but leaving you wondering what the particulars of your path really are.

From our nonlinear perspective we would view it as a basic interactive dimensional communication. You sense it internally but often find difficulty translating the message... the Whispers....those gems of wisdom emanating with intensity from the self from all the energies who know you well.

Sometimes in life you have need of a friend. Someone who can see you from all sides and dimensions. Sometimes, help is needed with the messages that come from spirit outside of your time line.

Welcome to "Inner Whispers"... a communication without boundaries from the nonphysical perspective.

You are the whispers... we are but the translators. Welcome."

-VERONICA

2

Satisfaction

"How often have you felt fully satisfied?

Often?

Sometimes?

True satisfaction within the self comes from the connection with your entity source.

Where you come from in physical is a result from where you originated eternally.

Complex?

No actually very simple.

Within the linear experience one often becomes enamored with the physical attributes of existence. Survival's attributes of existence. Survival's achievement and comfort become the seemingly clearer focus. As the soul develops through the body experience the physical moment falls flat without the higher parts of your self fully engaged.

This disconnect is felt deeply throughout the self leading to a sense of incompleteness.

Haven't you ever felt a void but could not define it?

The turbulence around you leaves you feeling powerless. The lack of satisfaction in your progress mounts until you are unable to function properly.

Should you despair?

No.

Find the eye of the hurricane where you originated from. By placing yourself in this space you can connect with your entity. The storm about you will be irrelevant.

Satisfaction exists only through this connection.

Start by identifying the core of who you are. You know who that is.

Why don't you let the energy out?

Satisfaction lies there.

Begin.

You're not alone.

The rest of you awaits.

There is no better company than the higher aspects of yourself."

-VERONICA

"Life is about *balance...*"

From VERONICA

3

The Question Most Asked

"How do I become more spiritual and more aware?

This is a question most often asked of our energy. In your desire to ascend to other levels of existence, it is important to remember that you designed this experience. The abandonment of all the issues attached to it will not in fact advance your energy without the experience.

If it's not going well... look at your contribution to that dilemma. It's often easier to blame others for the predicament. Difficult situations arise through your creation to resolve energies of current, past, and future. If you are discontented with your surroundings change it. However, that means that you have to change yourself.

Not an easy thought, is it?

Of course your initial reaction is to assign outside sources as the villain of whatever is occurring.

All we are saying is that you consider your input, alter it even slightly and see what occurs.

Whenever you change the ingredients of a situation the result will be different than the current one.

In essence we are saying that to become more spiritual and aware one should become more involved in the physical.

'Just a thought.

Consider the next time a situation leaves you feeling separated from your spirit and disgruntled.

Consider changing your approach. See what happens."

-VERONICA

4

Appreciating the Physical

"Often there is speculation that the physical state is one that should be abandoned or ascended from. Naturally the whole idea of existence is one of evolution. It does not simply occur in the physical.

We have heard "whispers" of the incarnated body as it passes from life to life. Your culture supposes that it is an existence of less and that the spiritual state is the ultimate moment.

May we suggest that the spiritual mind creates the physical?

In that moment the sense of touch becomes a pristine gift. Nowhere in the universe does it exist except in the skin of an incarnate soul. It should be appreciated as an advanced creation of the soul... It's existence manifested by a creation that will transcend the soul to higher realms.

The next time you curse your physical, hoping for a free pass to the eternal, we suggest you recall the utter awe of your fingertips as they caress the skin you now inhabit. The path can be as "heavenly" as the destination.

You will appreciate the physical much more after the experience. We were much like yourselves in our quest for the attainment of enlightenment. Imagine our surprise when once nonphysical, we realized the value of the body.

We relate our experience so that you may blend both moments for more advanced evolvement.

Consider it.

It may change how you proceed with this current linear."

-VERONICA

5

Thoughts

"Thinking is one of the daily aspects of linear living. Everything you participate with right down to the brand of toothpaste you use is a thought process. It's something you do automatically without understanding the grandness of what is occurring.

Every time you think of something it manifests itself into your daily routine. All occurrences and experience in linear are a result of your thoughts.

Often we are asked to define what will occur with one's life.

A more informative answer would be for us to ask the questioner what their thoughts include. Are they positive? Negative? Or are they a jumble of randomness with no direction? We find that the more troubled the individual is the more scrambled is their thought process.

Our advice is to understand how important thinking is.

If you are currently dissatisfied with your life for any reason take the time to examine your thoughts. If you are truthful with yourself you will be able to see the process that has brought you to where you are now.

How do you change it?

Start by carefully examining what you think about but more importantly how you think.

Consider it.

Your thought creates your reality.

Would it not be a comfort to change those things that are unsuitable for you?

It is within your power.

Thoughts are the most powerful tool in the universe and they are right there in your head.

-VERONICA

6

Getting What You Desire

"Often we are asked in readings the likelihood of a particular linear event. There is great attachment to these outcomes that are laced with deep desire.

Those seeking what they desire blame outside forces for the demise of their dreams. We counsel that everything is possible if one keeps their thoughts clear and concise without the additives of unnecessary drama and scattered focus.

If you are wanting to manifest a scenario then be sure your focus is clear and the intent pure.

Be truthful with yourself about the origins of your desire. Escapes from your true lessons will not manifest something that ultimately will not serve you, i.e., you may believe in your current moment that a linear experience will fulfill your ultimate desire. However, in the eternal moment you know that it is a distraction prepared by yourself.

So be eternally truthful when seeking a desire.

All of your thoughts will manifest to physical so be concise and direct especially with yourself. In this way you will get what you desire. The rub is that it must evolve your spirit in some way. If it doesn't it will not manifest. Your higher self will see to that."

-VERONICA

7

Why Talk To An Entity?

"One would wonder who we are. An energy without linear form with a desire to communicate through words. We understand how those firmly planted in this reality would have reservations to our intent.

"Once or twice" we have embodied our energy for our own personal evolution. We speak this with a smile as we count the multiple dramas that have led us to this communication. We offer a view point that exceeds the parameters of your current environment. Where you see the trees in the midst of the forest we see the leaves and why they have grown as they have.

We are not linear though we have experienced it many times. We are merely further along the path. Our intent is to expand all of us further.

A sense of familiarity encompasses all as we continue in conversation. Embrace the flow of connections as we continue to blend with your essence.

The universe and all of its parallels are but a brief moment. This moment may change all of your experiences and answer your deepest questions. It's all right to know us for it will lead you to knowing yourself.

Welcome friend......."

-VERONICA

8

Your Spirit Guides

"We are often asked the labels or names of particular spirit guides. It seems that most feel a present connection but are unable to identify the source. The attachment to labels leads the individual to a different perspective that does not lead to the ultimate connection with that which they seek.

Remember that your guides are often focused primarily in the nonlinear. Some of them have physical lives but more often than not they have only partaken of existence in a nonlinear form. This perspective is often unavailable to the current physical perspective and is often abandoned due to unavailability of a simple definition.

We suggest that instead of attempting to define the relationship in linear terms, one should attempt to deliver the vibrational connection to the self.

The message is not always a word based direction but rather an impulse of feeling that translates non-verbally to heighten your evolvement.

3 Steps to Your Guides

1. Use your senses to blend with the energy.

2. Attempt to detach emotionally from your ego so that the message has more clarity.

3. Trust yourself that your capabilities will provide what you need to hear in the moment.

As always, we are available to translate messages but the task is one that all can embrace.

Your guides speak continuously in hope of connection with you.

There is no blockage from their perspective."

-VERONICA

"Your guides speak continuously in hope of connection with you."

From VERONICA

"We communicate... to open your eyes: Spiritually and Physically...to another way of living"   --T

A Message from T

in "Parting Notes": A Connection With The Afterlife

9

Connection

"We suggest that a more accurate assessment is the return to the entity from which you have originated. From this particular energy there can be alignment with guides, spiritual advisers and friends who you know well.

When you participate in physical life the opportunity to create dramas for growth are abundant. In a conscious aware environment these dramas are placed appropriately and are easy to disengage from so that one can connect with the originating entity. However, in most instances the dramas become the higher source of energy and block any ability to realign with what you most desire.

Our advice is to learn to discern the irrationally created environments whenever possible. This can be done by understanding what you are creating & stopping the spiral of irrationality through complete honesty with the self.

Often this is extremely difficult but attainable. Quiet the arguments in your head, allowing the self to observe rather than experience, even for a brief moment.

In the silence recognize your true self, which will allow the connection without too much effort.

Once you do it, the rest will be easy, however, not comfortable. Do not expect that."

-VERONICA

10

Who Am I?

"In each lifetime there are issues that come to the forefront that can block the true intent of a life. Dramas unfold that seem to conflict with the thought process that appears to be attached to your soul. This often leads to distress as one feels the pull of intent against the linear reality of physical. The constant division of attention required by both leaves the individual exhausted and ultimately worried.... "Am I fulfilling the focus of my soul?

Let us begin by stating that there are no wasted lives. Assuredly dramas can block the progress, but if one is truly rational in their thinking process these things will manifest and fulfill themselves without hindering spiritual growth.

The trick is to recognize them for what they are and attempt not to be disillusioned by them but rather propelled by them.

Confusion results from the intensity of linear drama. It becomes a distraction when ultimately you feel the great void of "I am missing something here".

In the course of your life it is important to meet yourself head on. If you are anytime fearful you will create a distraction to "protect the ego yourself". The evolved moment occurs when you sense the distraction, embrace it, perhaps let it unfold but continue upon your true intent.

So in the quest for who you are remember, that as you move through your linear dramas, one must remain conscious. It is easier to become automatic, reacting and acting upon the moments created. Recall who is the creator. You. Recall that the more focus the more ability to pinpoint the creation of what and who you are.

Do not distract yourself through fear. Live through it but be aware.

The "Who am I?" will become apparent as you think through the moment. Dramas are dramas but they are merely an extension of yourself. Through conscious awareness the "Who am I?" becomes less of a mystery and more of a powerful auto-biography."

-VERONICA

"I was dead. Yet I still was. I had been mistaken... No matter what you think, there is more".

From: "Parting Notes": A Connection With The Afterlife

11

Remembrance

"As you move from one experience to another the lessons that you learn or don't learn go with you. Those who would be in alignment with you during these moments will indeed encounter you again.

Nothing is lost as one moves through the passages of life. Individuals who pulse in unison with your energy will indeed find you again.

In your culture there have been many descriptions of these encounters. Most of them inaccurate, some of them reminiscent of the cycle of life that is the truest.

Evolution cannot be attained through one drama or experience. All sides of the equation are desired in the examination of an issue. Thus multiple lives are often necessary to align with the oneness of spirit.

There is a faint pulse of energy, just enough for most to have slight memory. It may encounter you as you go about your daily routine. Just a whisper that feels like something more.

Remembrance.

Though you may have been taught of singular opportunity, it is actually more than that.

What a wonderful opportunity to get all the experience. You have many chances to get it right.

Remember.

The path is not a slight one. It is multifaceted with many inputs of information.

All that you have known, you will and do remember. Nothing is lost. You are a seed of god energy sent forth to know it all.

Remember."

-VERONICA

"Finding happiness does come with the decision to be so."
From VERONICA

12

The Eye of the Hurricane
(You are not alone)

"The dismay and frustration created by these experiences often lead to more disconnection and lack of Spirit in your life. It is necessary for you to understand that those in Spirit are always available. It is the distortion created by whatever linear actions that exist for you that give the appearance of separation.

The best way to describe it is to compare it to a storm or hurricane of events. The wind blows harder as you struggle to separate fact from fiction. As you spin out of control the sense of loss from your true spiritual identity can be devastating. The devastation can leave you vulnerable and seemingly separated from the source of creation.

If you feel this way it would be desirable to pause. Yes we said pause and realize that it is your web of physical drama that is causing all of it. Become quiet and removed from the drama. Step outside the hurricane carousel of events. Recede or proceed to the eye of the hurricane (whichever phrase resonates best with you).

Once you have paused it will be easier to identify the root of the problem. Allow all of the interactions, events, and un-fulfilling relationships that have been blinding you to the higher values of your true self and your spiritual guides to fall away. You have not been abandoned, merely distracted. Everyone who knows you are right there.

Those in Spirit await your pause. They have never given up hope that your attention to them would be revitalized.

Even if you feel the time has been long, to them it has been but a moment.... time being irrelevant in all Spiritual moments.

So seek "the eye" of whatever dilemma you are facing. All who love you are anxiously awaiting reunion.

You are not alone."

-VERONICA

"The Spiritual Connection is the ultimate experience.
It enhances all others...."
From: Reflections of a Spiritual Astronaut

13

The Calmness of Connection

"It does not matter where your focus is directed, the most common concern of those in physical is spiritual connection. 'Is it enough? Can I do more? Who are my guides? I feel them but the communication is scattered.'

"At times I feel so isolated!"

"What can I do?'

From a spiritual perspective we advise calmness. A belief system that includes all possibilities gives a limitless advantage to those who seek to connect with their spiritual counterparts.

In your physical environment most of you are caught in a whirlwind of activity and contrived progress. Some of your cultures are driven by physical success while others live in a virtual void of creativity.

Many religions promise evolution but lead most on a circular path to nowhere. The most intimate connection to the source of spiritual energy is within yourself. You are the map to inner consciousness that will lead to connection and your ultimate evolution.

Your guides whisper continuously in hopes of connection with you. In a frantic pace in physical it can be most impossible to connect.

The calmness of eternity where your soul originated is the best path to your desired reunion with all.

So calm down. Look about you. See what you've created and acknowledge why you have done so.
Breath deeply and appreciate how you have manifested in your current environment.

Calm.

Peaceful.

Omnipotent energy in physical form.

That's you.

Slow down and allow the magnificent energy of your soul to do its original intent.

Everyone is different in their purpose but all must be still from a moment to recall what it is.

This is the first step in answering all of your deepest questions.

Breath. Calm down."

-VERONICA

"A broken heart mends if the proper attention is delivered by the self to the self."

From VERONICA

14

Emotion

"Emotion is the shading, texture and color of an otherwise black & white experience in the physical. It is the explosive charge that ignites linear existence so that the impact is felt throughout all of your moments.

We realize that some will argue that it can be a hindrance to the intellectual perspectives of certain essences. We honor that position but retain the ultimate importance it will have somewhere in your journey no matter what your current belief systems may be at this moment.

There have been conversations with those incarnate who may have a misunderstanding of the potential of emotion. This may have sprung from a chaotic past experience or simply from a lack of partaking thus far.

Some essences are centered in emotion making their position more explosive in either a positive or negative fashion. We venture to state that from your perspective both ends of the poles can be beneficial in a well rounded physical experience. One life can be extremely positive while another the opposite in negativity. All sides of the coin are needed in a true perspective of emotion. Those centered thusly will whole heartedly agree.

Essences with a more intellectual perspective will choose to analyze emotion rather than experience it until they shape it into a more palatable perspective for themselves. So, for example, if you are less emotionally based than others in your current moment, that does not mean that you will never experience it properly. The definition is left to your own creations. We simply state all will experience it in their own fashion, in their own time.

There are those who also observe all the facets of emotion from an outside perspective. It does not limit the intensity of their experience so the judgment of another emotional barometer is inappropriate.

Again we repeat, it is the shading texture and color of a black & white physical experience. You are the artist who chooses the appropriate pallet for yourself. The brushes and canvases will be defined another day, another time."

-VERONICA

15

Transition

"We realize that there is expectation of a standard response that will alleviate the stress attached to the journey. It is however not standard by any means. It is as different for each individual as your differences of body type and process now.

Every soul imagines for its self its path back from whence they came. Issues and belief systems play a grand part of how the death process transpires for each individual.

It has been dramatized by those who remain physical but in actuality develops as a natural often subtle moment. So low key that most do not even realize what has occurred until there is intervention from guides and loved ones.

The destination varies according to the soul's evolution. A moment created by the self so that all lessons can be assimilated.

Realize that there is continuity to your existence. There will be remembrance of all and reunion. Those who know you well, will reunite with you.

It is not a finale...

merely..,

... intermission.

A moment of reflection on your path to evolvement. There may be more lives or not. It all depends on how well you lived this current moment and the lessons gleaned from it all.

It is a continuing journey.

Death is merely a pause to reflect on the progress of your eternal self so far."

-VERONICA

16

Purpose

"What is my purpose?

Who am I?

I forgot.

I thought I knew once but so many events blurred exactly what it was.

The confusion envelops you as the circular motion of blocked life force attempts to proceed on its course to a preconceived heaven.

What is heaven anyway?

...An often asked question about the utopia of the soul as it succeeds in its perceived tasks necessary for its evolution.

We venture to state that heaven is more of a state of soul accomplishment rather than a place of existence. It is a notion in the mind's eyes of the physical that dangles like a carrot in front of you on your way to salvation.

From a spirit perspective every moment of existence is a heavenly moment. Each event, death, birth, choice and conclusion is a gift and reward.

Your purpose universally is to evolve and be more than before. The details range widely through all experiences.

Individual purposes are revealed when you are ready to hear the truth. The truth resonates within you whether you choose to accept it or not. We have often relayed the personal truths of those who have asked, however, acceptance is not a natural given for most.

So if you are driven to reconnect with your purpose be prepared to accept the potential of it being a surprise that will later resonate within you.

Give it some thought.

As you connect, revelation will be imminent."

-VERONICA

17

A Moment Out of Time

"One of the most difficult moments for those in physical is the "enchainment" of time. The total involvement in the perception of time while leaving behind moments of introspection.

Most of you live by your clock. Run here, run there, the appointment calendar ever full and oppressive. The success of your physical defined by how much is accomplished within a life timeline.

The right education.

The successful job.

Beat the clock.

Beat the odds.

Become prosperous.

All defined by a time-line that does not really exist.

We suggest that if you are on the path of physical fulfillment, that there is a paused moment of reflection each day that reminds you of the true reality.

Infinite existence far surpasses a brief moment in physical.

Take time to reflect each day upon the vastness of consciousness, and the moment you are experiencing is just but a blip on the eternal moment. You are far more than your fingertips. Your thoughts extend beyond what occurred today and you are in charge of recreating those moments you were not so happy with.

Take time to think clearly. Without clear thoughts there is high probability of turmoil.

Take a moment out of your time-line to think and create clearly. slow down. Use thought wisely. It is your paintbrush... creating the tapestry of you.

Slow down.

Take time.

After all, time is yours.

Create wisely."

-VERONICA

Editor's Note: VERONICA tells me that the word "enchainment" as used in the first paragraph of her message above is a French word that essentially means "linked", or one link following another.

A Message from The Entity "T"

"There is great comfort in the familiarity of experience. A common ground that unites individuals in a way that is often felt energetically. Most of you have lived such a moment, either minimally or profoundly in the linear.

As one progresses through a life pattern, the pattern often becomes the reality focus rather than the soul intent. Thus by the total involvement in the drama the individual loses sight of the eternal perspective that put them in to the linear moment to begin with. This is very true of younger souls as they participate and sometimes even more evolved souls become enraptured by the physical linear dramas they participate in.

Those with a more expansive perspective often feel a profound difference between themselves and the others who are entrenched in physical.

We are not speaking to define anyone's linear moment. We speak only to raise consciousness of the ability to transcend the dramas of all who breathe in the physical.

Take a moment when wound tightly in a drama to realize who and what you actually are. An omnipotent life force that is capable of creating reality and ascension with a mere thought. It's possible to lose sight of that while participating in a progress of linear experience.

The difference between the two perspectives is remarkable when viewing it from our nonlinear perspective: The subject raised by our perception of what occurs moment by moment in your time frame. When in the eye of the hurricane the view is often more clearly defined.

We ask only for a moment of reflection to see your way clear. Stop briefly while the drama unfolds. You will see in the pauses that the drama has a life of its own and will continue without you.

Let it go.

It most likely will never miss your presence. It only needs your energy.

Without it, there will be a cessation of its existence.

Try it
and
see."

T

Editor's Note: "T" is a very highly evolved group entity that communicates with us only a few times a year.

18

No Separation

"The separation between those not physical and those who are is always perceived as grand by those in physical.

There is no separation, only reunion.

Those in Spirit Know.

Those in physical should reconsider their perceptions.

Those in Spirit grow louder in their communications.

Are you listening?"

-VERONICA

19

The Soul is the Source

"The soul is the source of the perception of self as it navigates through physical. There are many definitions but the driving force of soul creation while in spirit and flesh is the thought process. Thus whatever moment you find yourself in has been created by you. Therefore the conditions around you have not created the situation. You have created the conditions that place you where you are. Blaming the conditions will only serve to heighten their existence.

Being physical is a pristine gift. Nowhere in the universe is the sense of touch as felt through the fingertips available. Realize that even though the purpose of life may elude you at present, there is an intent from the soul that may have been blurred and distorted through inappropriate choices.

Return to your thoughts.

Rediscover your original intent.

The rediscovery occurs while thinking through and beyond the dramas.

It is possible.

First realize the beauty of your creation that is you.

Reconnect with the energy.

You have "thought" this experience before it began."

   -VERONICA

"There is no better company than the higher aspects of yourself."

From VERONICA

20

A Message From "T"
Who are you, really?

"There are different belief systems attached to the origin of man, most of them irregular while others are just plain inaccurate. Adhering to the policies of others often leaves one pondering aimlessly through a maze of definitions that fall short on an internal soul level.

The power of spirit is most often defined outside the self, painting a picture of omnipotent energy that an individual in human form should worship for bits of understanding and favor so that they may come to heaven profoundly.

While all of this may give comfort to younger souls, the more evolved ones find themselves at a loss for a real defined moment of accurate information.

The real test of humanity begins in the realization that God or the energy of creation is not an outside influence but rather a pulse of energy that resides in every soul, including you.

The magic of creation at any level begins in the thought process in everyone of the universe's beings.

The key to realization begins slowly. Your thoughts are experience and evolution waiting to occur both linearly and eternally. God does not exist outside of our current form. The energy exists in the hearts of all of you waiting patiently to manifest through your thoughts.

Worship is irrelevant.

Embracing the energy is more conducive to transcending to a higher place of understanding.

So, if your belief system includes a god why not blend completely and be a miracle instead of expecting one?"

T

21

Connection

We are often asked if this can be defined as a soulmate. In linear time the need for definition crowds the experience limiting the view point of the parties involved.

Energy is simply energy. When it has the same inception and vibrates with the same consistency it easily gravitates to familiar territory. The connection blends together recreating the environment from which both energies were formed.

From most linear points of view the connection appears to be a once in a lifetime opportunity. They do not take into consideration the dramatic moments enlisted by the energies to learn and evolve. Sometimes the exterior moments detour the connection for that current point in existence.

The so called disconnect from like energies occurs most often in this manner.

As disappointing as it may be, it would be better to understand that more than one energy intersection is possible in any given timeline.

The romantic notion of one and only has been enhanced through unrealistic perspectives.

So the answer to the soulmate question reveals itself to be a multiple if one adheres to all the energetic probabilities available.

Soulmates are not limited to male/female romances. They may also occur between female/female and of course pets within the time frame.

In the search for a perceived soulmate openness to all probabilities is warranted. Often the energy connection occurs without warning when both parties are engaged in a relaxed atmosphere. Most importantly be your true self. Another conversation will reveal the path to that moment.

Be open.

Be without opinion.

Be yourself.

You never know what your pure energy will attract."

--VERONICA

22

Everything Is Energy

"Most linear cultures view and discern their spiritual evolvement by linear standards. Belief Systems based in the timeline often paint a distorted viewpoint of that subject.

What we see is energy. The absence of a timeline in our experience offers us a full view of the individual. This moment allows us to access that energy giving them a viewpoint of themselves without time. By having this information one is better able to navigate through their experience.

Everything is energy. View spiritual progress as a vibrational one. The goal to perceived ascension is the heightened Spirit of energy: Your energy as it relates to the physical life you have manifested to understand that.

It pulses with a breath of physical and thoughtful creation of reality. It only appears to have linear levels.

Expand the place within you that knows the truth thus eliminating the go nowhere dramas that distract from your own energy."

-VERONICA

 **From ISH**

"We have a message:"

The day is wrought of many things
The past present and future
When it comes to what your life brings
It's all about your thoughts

You can blame the universe for being unfair
  and find comfort in idea of victim hood
Ultimately it is all about you and how you
  wear the choices presented to you by yourself

So take responsibility for the results

No matter if you like it or not
The measure of evolvement comes
from your ability to own your choices

Deal with it

Editor's Note: There is a considerable "back story" about Ish and his friend Osco yet to be told. However, Ish has been published in Omni Magazine and has written many interesting things.

"One must take responsibility for one's creations. And by taking that responsibility is the only way you can change them."
From: Madeline, an Entity and Guide

23

The Truth

"Fantasy of course feels better in the immediate moment but usually haunts the scenario of all parties until the truth is told. The damage of such events is often irreparable causing the choice making factors to spin out of control.

When incarnate the integrity of your actions & words are key to the evolution of your soul. Think not of immediate satisfaction but to the eternal progress of your soul. Without truth there can be no real progress. Rather a loop of fantasy that leaves your soul spinning endlessly in its pursuit of completeness.

Our counsel is that the truth may be uncomfortable. It may require braveness beyond what you think you are capable of. However, without it there is nothing but a limitless haze of drama that will unfold into the ultimate demise of the glass house you are living in.

Speak the truth.

Live the truth.

Claims of ignorance in regards to the truth are mere excuses made by individuals who are afraid.

The truth supersedes your current existence. It is the stepping stone to your ascendance.

Speak the truth.

Live the truth.

It's the best tool you have to work with to become who you really are.

Be not afraid.

The truth is your friend."

-VERONICA

24

The Purpose

"We have spoken to many who simply cannot recall what their purpose was for entering into their current life. They feel a sense of floundering that leaves them wondering why they incarnated at all... the goals attached to this seemingly long abandoned by what they perceive as themselves... dramas of their life often clouding any eternal sense of self while the ticking of time pulsates in their heads.

Some see no real conclusion to what they perceive as a useless and often painful existence... this due to the life path that is out of line with what their eternal self had planned in the beginning.

We counsel a slowing of the fast paced linear reality that most of you find yourselves in. A lack of focus upon the clock is the first step to understanding the larger portion of yourself that does not perceive time.

Physical existence is not a race to the finish. It is a participation in a reality that was meant to enlighten and fulfill your higher entity that wishes to evolve.

Slow down.

Take yourself when you are able to a quiet place. Your thoughts cannot create your reality with all the chaos.

Slow down.

Take a moment to ponder yourself without time increments and deadlines.

In this place of quiet the whispers of your soul will have opportunity to speak.

This is the first of many steps that we will speak of on your way to rediscovering yourself.

Slow down."

-VERONICA

25

The Value of a Clear Mind

"We have memory of physical and all that that entails. The dramas that are created from the most simple endeavors leaving the brain muddled from all the intense input.

It is important for the reader to understand that we comprehend quite well what it is like to incarnate. The overwhelming scenarios that leave your thoughts compressed in such a way that there seems to be no clear path to redemption available. An excess of negativity clinging to your body like a shroud, leading it seems nowhere but to worse enactments. Yes we see it. Yes we feel it for we have experienced such moments.

A clear perspective might have changed everything. Opportunity might have at least eased the burden we felt so acutely at that time.

What would we have told that linear existence from our now clear eternal view?

What indeed?

The most important thought in such a dramatization is that though it may feel you are out of control it is not necessarily so.

Your thoughts are your greatest gift and your most useful tool.

It's easy to succumb to defeat. Letting yourself become victim to negativity is often a self interpreting moment. Most are not clear enough in thought to be self interpreting therefore they give up and become a part of the whole negative picture.

If you find yourself in despair a moment or perhaps more of clarity of the mind would be prudent.

Examination & acceptance go hand in hand with the truth. So if you find yourself in a predicament, keep your thoughts in focus. It's really the only weapon you have.

Slow down.

Think

Embrace the thoughts.

Implement the thoughts without constricting fear base moments.

Thought without fear = power.

-VERONICA

From Ish

a few words may be not
we told you once and you forgot
how to make the world go round
stepping softly without a sound
events are fleeting and often we find
there's more to a moment with your kind
look to each action as if it were gold
you are a child of the cosmos and very bold

remember this always and state your place
others will know and respect your space
the universe is giving to those who take
and a menace to all who do not make
a stand and defend their right to create
exactly what they speculate
to be heaven

(from your personal cheering section in the cosmos)

Editor's Note: As with all of the nonphysical beings that either dictate or write material for "Inner Whispers", the message from Ish above and all of his material is printed exactly as typed by him (Ish prefers typing to speaking or writing in long hand) in first, final, and only draft. There is zero editing of any of his work. It is exactly how it came out on the screen, one letter... and then one word... at a time... with Ish using just one finger on each of the trance channel's hands to type.

26

The Size of the Ego

"As the eternal soul seeks evolution and experience, it encounters and inhabits the linear physical body.

As in all partnerships there is a give and take between the energy. The spiritual side often labeled as the soul has an agenda to perceive life lessons, pursue them and to make great strides to resolve them. The physical form with ideas of its own, perceives the soul but then becomes very attached to the "me" of the moment... Forgetting other lives in the identification of the self as it dwells in the current physical form.

It depends upon the evolution of the soul how much the ego plays into the plan of enrichment the soul has planned.

It is extremely difficult to separate the identification of the self when the soul is new to the idea of incarnation and the opportunity it offers.

Younger souls often completely embrace the current life as the one and only opportunity. In doing so there can be a complete abandonment of eternal sight or a concentrated one that clings to the idea of salvation from one experience.

The idea of self within physical form is indeed a three dimensional process. The size of an ego may vary but ultimately it is merely a singular reflection of your soul and the entity you came from.

The ego being finite becomes fearful without the soul's infinite perspective. Religion plays upon this perspective so that the ego may follow a path of comfortable salvation, which indeed appeals to the eternal soul.

-VERONICA

27

Culture as it Relates to Infinity

"Energy as it manifests in the linear can be related to in many different ways.

A proponent of this manifestation can translate quite differently through different cultures. The physical experience has many directions, it can go through all of them so differently it is difficult to summarize by words.

We can tell you that all physical experience whether positive or negative translates differently from culture to culture. This enables much growth eternally while enabling the culture to manifest itself accordingly... to the individual spiritual plan.

We are not hoping to confuse but to put a fine definition upon the experience while linear.

The opportunity to evolve while engaged in multi diverse cultures is indeed a gift. This gift enables a broad perspective for energies to design their own path to ascension.

Now if you are currently linear this may appear broad and indefinable, but if one truly desires evolution it is necessary to be this way.

Embrace your perspective, honor the culture. The culture does not have to define the ultimate moment but it is indeed an ingredient to all of it.

In the linear it is often mistakenly defined as the one and only way. In an eternal perspective this is often inadequate.

So we say embrace the culture but allow for the other experiences to have their say.

All in all it is the combined experience of culture that ultimately will make a difference.

We understand the inadequacy of this dissertation, however, it will be fruitful to embrace the multiplicity of all of it.

-VERONICA

Editor's note: This particular article was done by several entities that were "blending" with VERONICA as she wrote it. The experience for me was quite different than talking with VERONICA alone. VERONICA told me that there were 17 entities in this particular blend. ~Allen

28

In Sickness and in Health.....
It's All About What You Think
and Experience.

"In physical form one daily creates the dramas and images that propel the soul through a linear experience. It is the perspective of the soul to manifest a "Garden of Eden" that will bring forth the ideals of the spirit as it progresses on its way to understanding all aspects of itself.

Along the way there may be disappointments that occur that will misalign the body out of line with the intent of the soul. This can lead to an uneasiness within the physical form that will manifest into linear Illness.

The way to progress beyond the ailments is to align one's thought patterns to wellness and easiness of the mingling of spirit & flesh. Thoughts create everything in a life. By aligning with the illness and its pitfalls one will continue to bring forth more illness.

Better to visualize the prosperity of the intent of the soul to become well. By this we do not mean that in a progressed moment there will suddenly be healing. Often illness is an accumulation of many lifetimes of disjointed energy that manifest repeatedly until more positive thinking & being is introduced to the physical form inhabited by the spirit.

The way to wellness is to be clear of all distractions & to see the truth of what truly is occurring.

There is no victim hood attached to the progression of illness through many lifetimes. Remember that your body is merely a reflection of your soul. Ease the soul and uncomfortableness in the flesh will be greatly reduced.

Illness is uncomfortable.

To leave physical form due to illness is unnecessary.

However, it is up to you to rearrange your thought process to include a place of refinement where one can exist in a "Garden of Eden". This place remains in all thought regardless of culture. It is the ultimate union of body & spirit not known to all but indeed available.

Attempt clear thought."

-VERONICA

# From ISH

Up until i was three

it's always was my dad and me

no matter what was tossed our way

our bond was solid

our life was gay

struggle was constant, but we didn't care

peanut butter 'n jelly, macaroni and cheese

our bond was solid

our life was a breeze

as i turned six i asked about her

the one who caused anger to occur

she wasn't important that's what he said

our bond was solid

she was practically dead

on my eighth birthday there was a surprise

my dad met a woman with hazel eyes

he said that he needed another adult

our bond was solid

who would know the result

of a cold hearted woman that hated me so

twisted my father 'till i didn't know

if he still loved me and wanted me there

our bond was solid

so she didn't dare

try to get rid of me before i was nine

i saw right through her chronic whine

so did my dad to my relief

our bond was solid

my one true belief

when i was ten i started to see

how dad was dreadful to his own family

it seemed to be centered upon the female part

our bond was solid

be silent my heart

now i'm eleven and quite a child

my impact on father is hardly mild

holding on still to my one true love

our bond is solid

till push comes to shove

for all the years i've known my dad

there's only one thing that makes me sad

you see way deep in my heart i know for sure

our bond is solid

it will always endure

however i know in my deep subconscious

my dad hates women that's why he's obnoxious

to female members both family and friend

our bond is solid

it will never end

tomorrow i'll play ball with dear old dad

and look back at all the fun we've had

we'll laugh and laugh and put on a show

our bond is solid

i simply won't grow

(found in a diary of a young female on the verge of
womanhood)

29

What is Real

"We are asked occasionally if we are real. We suppose this question emanates from the incarnate spirit who does not remember the origin of itself.

To define "real" we are not in physical form at the present time. This does not, however, define who we are. We have been many physical forms in an attempt at an evolution process that is indeed multi-dimensional.

Multi-dimensional does not translate easily to the linear mind set. Since we have been linear we understand where the question comes from.

Anything not defined by the parameters of physical needs an element of faith so ascribed to by many religious organizations of our created reality.

Faith is blind but the pulse of an inner knowing and memory sends most incarnates on a quest for the infinite that even they cannot define. It just is.

Those who align themselves to spirit often find religious faith un-fulfilling thus seeking something "real".

We are as real as you are in the current moment. We simply are at a different vibratory pulse... the physical no longer an avenue of evolvement for us.

All of you will be in this moment ultimately... some sooner than later. Since we are not incarnate we are able to read the energy of those we encounter. We are fortunate to have found a like energy to speak through [April Crawford].

We are as real as your dreams and dreams do come true if you decide they will.

Our place is merely a different perspective, embrace it or not.

We offer connection if you seek the infinite. It is where we reside and we invite you to an interchange of thought.

We are as real as your thoughts and dreams, manifested through a vehicle known as April."

-VERONICA

# From ISH

if i could

blot out the nightmare of existence

i would

let the children dream of heaven

if i could

eliminate starvation

i would

feed it to the lion of despair

if i could

stop all the nuclear reactions

i would

blow them into another dimension

if i could

stop all the needless suffering

i would

teach the gift of blessed creation

if i could

capture all the polluted air

i would

put it in a bottle

if i could

ease all the troubled souls of the earth

i would

feel my birth was successful

(thoughts of a newborn)

"The Universe has not created you, you have created
the Universe. You need to ponder that..."
From: Madeline

30

<u>Change</u>

"We have been asked most often the formula for changing the course of one's life. Change is a variable in a singular life that will alter circumstances for the better or worse. The core of change exists in all incarnate souls, however, it is most perceived as an external device. This is unfortunate in the regard that the changes desired often do not manifest in the way one had desired in the onset.

The only path to true change of any kind is to first change yourself. This can be as simple as a thought process or as complex as a life pattern.

Those who participate with you in linear will not change in accordance with your thoughts for they usually have no idea what your thoughts are, they only perceive their own.

Therefore, the only useful tool for change within your command is in yourself. If you feel unsatisfied with the current moment examine the thought process that led you there. Alter it and see where it takes you. Those who participate with you will either adjust or excuse themselves to your energy.

Of course it takes a certain amount of bravery to adjust yourself to your own path. Change in fact can be frightening if you are uncomfortable with yourself. Change eliminates those no longer appropriate to your current condition.

We caution expectation of change in others, they are merely reacting to your own energy. The path to change is indeed within you.

Once your change yourself to your liking, everything else will indeed manifest. It just takes courage to enlist your own energy.

Be brave and change yourself. All will alter accordingly."

-VERONICA

31

Names of Spirit Guides and Entities

"Energies who have clear remembrance of linear existence tend to indulge the individuals in physical who speak with them by offering a familiar name. In other instances the physical individual will simply entertain a comfortable label for reference purposes.

All in all the name label is never as enlightening as the conversation occurring between the two points of existence.

In our own consciousness there have been many names and circumstances from which we draw experience. To ascribe to one would not have been our choice. The name

Veronica was chosen by our linear friends early on as a reference point for their own identification.

The idea of linear simply does not translate to existences not focused in a time line. The term "there is no time" is an accurate assessment by those energies like ourselves. It is a system set in place by physical not spiritual.

Time is a perception of the physical not a constant in eternity.

We respond by narrowing our focus to your experience. While doing so we are able to assess your energy and deliver guidance as how to approach it. This is what we do."

-VERONICA

"The idea of just a single life opportunity would be
disappointing, for the sum of one life would not have
allowed for our total evolution..."
From VERONICA

32

Do We Exist?

"If one defines existence by linear parameters we indeed do not exist. By this we mean that we are currently not in a time line that defines our experience by a physical assessment.

We have full experience of all our lives at our disposal if we so choose. Access is immediate, while the enrichment of the knowledge propels us ever more expansively on our journey to fulfillment. The definition of this fulfillment is a unique pilgrimage set forth from the entity from which we were cast.

While a physical life is pristine in its moment, a full encounter with the self could not be fulfilled by a singular experience. An example of such could be defined by the idea of interest in a particular linear subject. By reading or experiencing the subject an accurate assessment could not theoretically be attained until one either read all the material available or participated in as many experiences as possible within the subject matter.

Such is evolvement of the soul."

-VERONICA

33

Time for The Soul

"The briskness of living leaves one breathless in the pursuit of the true purpose for incarnating. We are often questioned on the "why" of one's existence in a particular life process while the true desire of the soul appears to have been left behind or misplaced.

There is great sorrow when one feels they have lost their way. Whispers of the path sometimes echo in the mind but the chaos of daily living and survival suppress the opportunity for clarity.

We have spoken to many of the frustrated individuals seeking "to right" the seemingly wrong turns of their life processes. For the soul to blossom in a linear life there is need for focus and reflection without the interference of drama.

We feel the tenseness in your energy as you read this. The voice in your head immediately lists many reasons for the disconnect you feel from the world of the eternal. Your work, relationship, children, family, etc. all have priority in the immediate moment for your attention. There seems nothing left, and you are correct.

The soul needs nurturing more than any other element in your life. Everything else will eventually suffer without a solid connection to your soul and yourself.

Yes, others have need of you but without your inner soul's energy they will be unfulfilled.

You have to have it to give it, in other words. Time for the soul is the best path to fixing the misaligned life you feel dissatisfied with.

So what does one do to reconnect with the soul? Give it time & attention so that it may communicate with you as intended when you decided upon a physical life.

Begin by taking some moments in your morning and before you retire to clear your mind of all the dramas of the day.

Give yourself permission to be still and tell others that you are meeting with your soul. Begin slowly & realistically. Be comfortable in those moments but most of all seek yourself, you know the one. The one you never have time for... your soul.

Attempt the process. You may be surprised at the results"

-VERONICA

# From ISH

anxious makes the mind grow weaker

worry a useless game

brashness a mask for those much meeker

than i'd like to name

all these labels tend to hide

the essence of the soul

costumes and roles provide a ruse

to achieve a certain goal

perhaps one should take a look

at what these goals should be

too bad there's not a golden book

to define our paths so we'd see

all the circus clowns we play

as our lives progress
you'd think we'd want more to say
and alleviate the stress
simply stop the wheels from turning
say no to another game
life is about the learning
no drama leads to fame
there's only you in the front row
no audience to cheer
alas my dear there is no foe
only you and your fear
the only path home is truth
and truth has no flair

(advice from a former drama queen)

34

(Inspiration)
Spirit Guides
How to Find Them

"We are often asked by those such as yourselves the path to meeting and identifying spiritual guides.

Each of you have a purpose in your current lives that beckons the heart but appears to be indefinable. In some cases your guides in spirit attempt contact but cannot speak clearly through the multiple chatters in your linear thought processes. The names are not necessary but the contact of energy often aligns the soul so that one is able to continue more in tune with the inner purpose.

Some of you feel their presence, others become frustrated because they do not. All incarnate souls are accompanied by energies that are not physical. They offer clarity compassion and focus if one is able to connect with them. Some are aligned at birth while others come and go as the need for their expertise ebbs & flows.

Never will they abandon the soul they have chosen to guide. If there is a feeling of less it is usually because the soul in question is out of sync.

The best way to align can be defined in there linear steps.

1. Realization that the connection is faulty due to the chatter in you own thought process.

2. A quieting of thoughts is completely necessary. Stop all the chatter by calming your linear.

3. To calm the linear, spend quiet moments with yourself. Be kind to yourself while asking for guidance. Give permission to the self to be nurturing to the self.

Your guides will never and have never abandoned you. Their love is eternal as is their interest in your evolvement. Open your silent mind to them. Realize that they have been patiently waiting for any kind of opening.

Shhh! Quietly.

Often they whisper."

-VERONICA

35

Belief Systems

"Every existence in the physical participates in a belief system that becomes relevant or irrelevant to the soul as it progresses.

There is no judgment from our perspective of which system perpetuates evolvement or not. Each experience is designed to bring clarity. Since the soul energy is unique and omnipotent it is only natural that there would be a variety of choices for every soul in every lifetime.

It is important for all souls incarnate to recognize the uniqueness they possess by existing in the physical. The honoring of other soul choices should not be excluded on the path to individual evolvement. As proven often in your physical sciences, energy frequency is varied and multi-tiered in its intenseness. It is only natural that there would be many approaches to the alignment of the core energy from which one emanates, i.e., the source of your soul.

Questions have been posed as to the origin of our energy. We are as yourselves only not continuing the physical line. Our perspective is a bit broader due to the lack of linear drama often created on the way to understanding in physical.

We seek not to pontificate on the path you should take. We merely offer perspective on the truths you really already know & which you may have forgotten... or perhaps misinterpreted.

There is not a correct single belief system since there are many varied consciousness souls currently involved in physical. These systems are usually derived from culture, and serve the individual in their numerous lessons and perspectives.

Religion in its linear form also can shade the beliefs of an individual. We only remind you to seek the truth of your soul, not the outside dogma and ceremonies attached to a particular religious venue.

Always seek the energy of your soul. If indeed a particular path calls you then be where you must be. Eventually the truth of eternity will find you, until then simply listen to your soul.

The voice of the inner will always be the clear one regardless of the volume of the many."

-VERONICA

36

The Intent of the Soul

"The energy that is you seeks the purpose of every linear life that it creates. We often are asked the purpose behind the creation of one's physical self. The intent of existence [is] often lost amongst the multiple confusing dramas created by the ego of the physical.

The muddled energy behind all these dramas sends mixed messages to the conscious self creating confusion for the individual who is truly engaged in finding the reason for their current existence.

'What is my purpose?'

The soul knows its intent but the ego attached to the physical manifestation becomes enraptured with the experience and loses all focus upon its original intent.

Those who wish to engage their soul should perhaps stop focusing upon their physical dramas and beckon a silent moment void of talk, movement or sound: The silence of all moments that shout different perspectives & expectations of a linear self that no longer adheres to the wishes of the soul.

This separation is the seed of all discontent with the physical. Unfortunately all who seek guidance with their purpose are often at the precipice of revelation. The ego, however, desperate to maintain its dominance will participate in any way it can to save its hold upon the individual.

'What do I do?' The ever present question of those seeking evolvement.

What to do indeed...

The best prescription is silence. Silence of all those ego based moments that resound in your heart & mind leaving you confused & desperate.

The soul was cast from a symphony of silence while all those in attendance joined in chorus, but it is the silence of ego that propels it to manifestation.

All the voices of your physical self taking a moment of silence while engaging the vocals of your soul will lead you to an understanding of your purpose.

It is not as you imagined it. It is not an event but an intricately woven tapestry of many lives that may or may not crescendo in your current life. Understand that in the end it is your soul intent that will prevail. Silence your ego and the path will become more available but not necessarily final.

Realize that physical life is a stairway to your enlightenment on a soul level. Each step important but it takes many steps to reach the next level. To judge your footsteps only impedes your process. Focus upon the stepping towards the goal, which is the reuniting with your intent & soul.

Progress occurs every moment, it just may not seem so from your current perspective."

-VERONICA

# From ISH

deep within my heart i know

it's often painful when we grow

into another chapter of this life

filled with anger and with strife

the passage should be smooth and clear

the way is possible and very near

so sit down beside me while i speak

very close now my voice is weak

let me whisper the secret of living

while i'm still in the mood for giving

the answer that you desperately need

in this world of poverty and greed

in all the time i've spent this time

the best were the ones that i could rhyme

the balance of words gave my soul a lift

perked up my senses when i needed a shift

out of my self created misery and pain

cleaned out the chakras and kept me sane

the answer you see is crystal clear

find one thing that you hold dear

and in that one thing that gives you pleasure

you'll find an everlasting treasure

so sit still my friend and close your eyes

block out the world and all its lies

see into the center of what is you

before long you'll see it too

the one thing that makes it fun

and worth a million when all's said and done

my talent and as i said this particular time

was to fill the world with witty rhyme

its made the difference in where i'm at

and will certainly determine where i am after that

so sit close beside me and let your self go

i guarantee you'll feel a flow

do it now and don't hesitate

do it now before it's too late

life slips by quickly and it's suddenly gone
do what your heart tells you before the dawn
of another life approaches.

(advice from my 98 year old grandmother before she died)

37

Nurturing the Self

"It is important while participating in a time line to take the time to nurture the self. There are many energies needing yours to navigate through their dramas. At the end of the day most of you feel depleted of the life force that ignites your own evolution. Your energy in a depleted state may cause mishap in the daily course.

We suggest a moment of contemplation whereas the personal energy of your own soul & physical can be recharged. The responsibility of others becomes over whelming when there's nothing left internally to be given.

It is not selfish to nurture the self. In fact it is the greatest giving to others because you actually have something to give. The exhaustion of such action may lead to depression and anxiety, leaving those who truly need your guidance void of any support.

Be kind to your self. Allow personal moments of comfort that lead to powerful replenishing. If you wish to love and nurture others your only recourse is to nurture the self."

-VERONICA

"No matter what you think,

there is more."

From: "Parting Notes": A Connection With The Afterlife

"William and I have traveled a long road to be together for eternity... not all of it blissful. Some of it was deeply painful; however, all of it was worth it.

We are now together for eternity. The blending of our essence crescendos in a space of existence that we always had searched for, but did not find, until now.

So we write this story so that those of you who are interested can see the progression of a love affair between soulmates as it spans through many lives of evolution, culminating in the final commitment we now share."

From: Sophia about her many lifetimes with William.

38

Matters of the Heart

"There are moments in life where the heart takes a bruising especially in the areas of relationships. These experiences have the ability to propel an individual into an evolvement stage, or into a negative spiral, which attracts more drama and more bruising.

We are often asked why, by those who seek counsel. It appears to those involved in a negative spiral that indeed their whole existence is out of control.

We suggest that if you find yourself in such a situation that a moment of pause may be useful. By this we mean to stop the energy that has created you into such a disheartening situation. Realize that the ideal formula for change is as simple as changing your own energy in the relationship. Often heart bruisings by another are an accepted fact by the recipient of the abuse.

There is no magic formula for changing others. One cannot create an elixir to change another's perspective in any relationship. All one can do is change their own perspectives.

Like a pebble thrust into a pond the ripples emanating from its contact forever changes the energy of the water, thus changing the dynamics of the pond.

If you are dissatisfied with any relationship we suggest digging deep into your own heart and energy to change it. Like a pebble, your actions from that change of perspective will make a difference.

After all it is all about energy. If you alter yours the surrounding energies adjust accordingly, some even falling away.

Realize that in the arena of the heart you are in just as much control if you embrace your power within yourself.

You can eliminate bruising and attract a fresh moment of prosperity in the relationship arena. You again must decide without fear. Move your energy around and watch the results.

If you are doubtful proceed anyway. There is nothing to lose. Just do it."

-VERONICA

From ISH & T Group

inside my head
there is a an empty
space
reserved for me alone

retreating there
i must admit
takes courage

it is clearly an act
of god
that i survive
the sweet embrace
of the solitude

in wonder
i step aside my fears
knowing them
for who they are

half the battle
of a busy life
is knowing
the real enemy

yes i retreat
to this empty space
to hold that which
holds me back

it gazes
at my reflection
so distinct

one ponders the universe

when all

the while the

universe is hiding

in that empty space

in you...

39

The Dearly Departed

"The loss of a loved one leaves many in physical isolated and alone. Depression may result from these feelings, which can broaden the perceived emptiness. It is important to maintain the knowledge that there is continuance. Your loved ones do indeed know that you grieve. It can be difficult for them because they still have complete awareness of you while those left in physical feel the door has been closed forever.

Know that the entrance to the spirit world is effortless once the body is discarded. A great feeling of emancipation accompanies many crossings from a body that is no longer functional and confining. Every experience is unique unto that particular energy, so there is no standard to the definition.

'Does he/she know that I miss him/her?' Yes and the intention of his/her thoughts are always to send you a message. Often he/she feels successful but there are moments when he/she senses that the opportunity was not embraced and the moment missed.

We suggest that if you have lost a loved one that you still your grief as much as possible. The moment of connection is often brief since the loved can no longer manipulate physical environments the way they did before. The ascent into spirit heightens the senses of the departed encouraging them to seek out opportunities of connection. It may take linear time for them to figure out how their new spirit 'reality' works.

Be patient.

Be still.

Pay attention to the small moments. They are often filled with messages from the departed that are more subtle than one would expect. In the beginning it may be more difficult for them because they are in the process of remembering what it means to be nonphysical. It is a more fluid environment and communication skills may be altered from what they previously knew.

The first moments might be a mere whisper in the wind that will crescendo into a cascade of communication.

Be patient.

Pay attention.

The dearly departed are whispering. They are still dear and close to you. It's just that they are now of spirit.

Pay attention.

Set aside your grief and know they are still there. Feel their love and their messages.

Look around for they are indeed everywhere."

-VERONICA

From ISH & T Group

my name is not important

least of all to you

i wake each day to nothing

hopes and dreams are few

once i was very thoughtful

my heart held no hate

that was before my loving father

decided to set me straight

get out of the way you idiot!

was my greeting from the crib

shut up and stop your crying

i didn't break your rib

yes my daddy loves me

he's just a bit confused

didn't mean to hurt me

and i'm certainly not abused

my name is not important

you see me every day

sometime soon i'll be older

perhaps my child will say

he didn't mean to hurt me

and i'm certainly not abused

yes my daddy loves me he

is just a bit confused

my name is not important

you see me everyday

some day soon i'll be older

perhaps my child will say

he didn't mean to hurt me

and i'm certainly not abused

yes my daddy loves me he

is just a bit confused

my name is not important

you see me every day

some day soon i'll be older

perhaps my child will say

he didn't mean to hurt me
and i'm certainly not abused
yes my daddy loves me he
is just a bit confused
my name is not important
you see me every day
some day soon i'll be older
perhaps my child will say
he didn't mean to hurt me
and i'm certainly not abused
yes my daddy loves me he
is just a bit confused
my name is not important.............

(a negative self worth issue can be repetitive.....be careful!)

"How you experience death is linked mostly with your emotional and spiritual state at the time of death..."

From: "Parting Notes": A Connection with the Afterlife

40

Inner Flame

"At the inception of the soul to the physical body a plan of action is instilled in the psyche of the individual. This plan evolves slowly within until it becomes a flame of power within the individual.

This flame is representative of the intent of the individual's soul. If it is not addressed or implemented it will smolder in the consciousness of the individual as something incomplete in their hearts.

The experience in physical can offer much distraction from this flame. Physical survival leads the progression followed closely by dramas and issues. Linear while being an intense focus often leaves the soul a sense of incompleteness if the inner flame is not addressed. The distractions of the linear may offer some respite from the flame but ultimately the intensity will come to the forefront as "I am missing something".

This sense of lack can derail the intent of the soul as it searches for linear solutions when the real issue is the satisfaction of the soul."

-VERONICA

41

Giving

"We are often asked how to regulate the amount of energy to give in the physical world. There are individuals in everyone's linear that would take from you until there was nothing left to give. It is important to understand the fine line between giver and enabler.

The giver provides energy to those who would need an energetic helping hand while they embark upon evolutionary endeavors. The path highly defined by their progress and continued cycle of giving by themselves to a continued chain of others.

The enabler gives unconditionally however the receivers sometimes use the energy to provide themselves with a stagnant moment of linear and repeat the same level of lack within themselves that caused the need for a helping hand to begin with.

If there is clarity in this process the giver would need no prompting upon where they fall in the definition. The desire to give is compelling, only be aware of the receiver and how the energy is applied.

The forward linear moments of accomplishment instead of repetitive cycular actions should be acknowledged by the giver before further energy is given.

Keep the mind clear and focused. The only opportunity of giving energy is that it is used for evolution not for continued negativity."

-VERONICA

"By depriving those negative ones of your energy, they will ultimately have no place to go but back to themselves..."

From VERONICA

42

Changing Negative Experiences

"In the physical one creates everything. The responsibility of one's reality can be overwhelming especially if one is feeling defeated by circumstance. There is not a single person who wishes ill upon themselves, however, in the storm of negativity it is imperative to get to the center of the difficulty to determine exactly what thought process brought you to this unfortunate place.

The first item to investigate is how your energy has participated. Of course the acknowledgement of that can be difficult especially if one is interested in their victim hood.

Secondly, the consideration of a remedy thought process that would begin to reverse or ease the current situation. This again can be problematic if the individual in question is comfortable in their current energy patterns.

Lastly, the patience required to change a negative reality can be disappointing. However, it is imperative to consider the weaving of thoughts that have created this unfavorable place. The worse it is, the more time it took for it to be created.

Patience again is essential as one proceeds to unravel a reality that is no longer valid.

Start then with yourself. As your energy changes and the alignment of better thoughts proceed, the surrounding environment has no other recourse than to change with you. Places, People and Problems will alter as you re-create yourself.

-VERONICA

"Change comes from the strength, and growth, and
awareness, of *conscious choice.*"

From VERONICA

43

Your Future

"We are often asked for predictions of the linear future. It is always of interest to us the lack of knowledge surrounding the subject. The ideas of fate or predetermined dramas with solid results are inaccurate ones at best.

Since we have been linear the idea of destiny is not foreign. However, in our current perspective the idea of a choice-less predestined life falls flat in our idea of living. This would be a great robbery of individual thought and soulful evolution.

From our memory the best lives lived were the ones where our choices garnered extreme experience. Each moment of decision a great gift that resulted in a life well done.

Of course there is an energy that creates probabilities that are planned by yourselves that result in your future, but it's the choices you make that result in your future.

What does this do?

Why it creates your path, custom designed to your specifications.

It is therefore critically important to you as a manifest energy to choose with clarity as you proceed through your linear.

The future is your tapestry.

Choose wisely."

-VERONICA

44

Deciding to be Happy

"In the linear life many obstacles occur to diminish the quality of experience that most aspire to. Out of ignorance or lack of focus that which we most wish to occur does not or becomes somewhat elusive in its blending into our lives.

The decision to be happy occurs at many levels. An abrupt close to the surface one [i.e., a decision to be happy] usually results in failure because of the lack of introspection involved. Happiness is not something that is available upon a whim. It is a thought process that begins internally at an unconscious level triggered by an emotional desire in the conscious level.

In many cases the definition of happiness currently employed by your psyche is inaccurate and delusional. It is important to understand that the decision to be happy consciously also embraces the idea well beneath the conscious level.

The layers of drama associated with your current life often blur the true seed of happiness within yourself.

Again, finding happiness does come with the decision to be so. Often it is not what you thought it would be at all. We suggest that if you find yourself forever out of touch with happiness that you stop whatever pattern you are creating and be still for a moment. Simply by stopping the flow of energy there will be a moment of clarity where the fog will lift.

Your energy always has the focus of happiness at hand. One simply has to be truthful about the definition of that happiness. Allow your soul to emerge to the surface of this current linear life. If nothing else is working what is there to lose besides the abundant unhappiness that you are currently experiencing?"

-VERONICA

"When you feel young, you become young..."

From "Reflections of a Spiritual Astronaut"

45

Broken Hearts

"Relationships while linear are volatile and sometimes disappointing. This imbalance of energy can leave the individual who gives too much energy a sense of incompleteness that is devastating.

It is important to understand the "energy" involved in every relationship and how balance is the key to it all.

We receive many letters written by souls whose linear hearts have been shattered by the imbalance of energy between them and another. One's voices range from the young inexperienced to those who are seasoned by multiple life experiences.

"Like always attracts like". If you are involved with another who wounds your heart the most important thing to do is to revive your own personal energy. The more broken your heart the more you may attract negativity. This is not to say that the other individual bears no responsibility. It merely suggests that the value of your worth is determined by yourself.

To allow another to diminish that may be acceptable once if you are seeking experience.

However, to allow such energy exchanges to continue reflects upon the opinion you have of your energy.

In most cases it is highly doubtful that the other energy involved will change it's pattern. It is up to you to examine and realign your own [energy] .

Consider that the relationship may have been created by your higher self for just that reason... to know your worth and to discover your own potential.

A broken heart mends if the proper attention is delivered by the self to the self.

-VERONICA

46

Path to Personal Power

"In the linear one often becomes intertwined in the dramas of daily life. Those moments have potential of expanding beyond the imagination of those who create them. Thus the feeling of overwhelming despair when one finds themselves in the midst of the storm.

It is important to recall yourself in a singular way devoid of all the energy interaction of others. Your own moment of consciousness may be able to override all the turmoil co-created by you and others.

Take a breath, separate your energy, realize that this moment is an opportunity to control your environment instead of becoming victim to it.

A co-creation is powerful but a concentrated personal thought can override the moment. Be firm in your moment. You are an omnipotent energy manifested in the flesh to evolve.

This evolution is your personal path to power within your own soul. Own it. Do not eliminate out of hand the opportunity simply because in a linear perception all appears to be lost.

It is not the case.

You can change the course of energy.

Simply stop.

You are a powerful energy manifested in physical through the eyes of eternal energy.

Simply stop.

You are more powerful than you can imagine. Your soul seeks the path of evolution.

Simply stop and acknowledge. The rest will manifest according to that.

All it takes is the moment to let go of the turmoil and return to your soul's eternal.

-VERONICA

**"Take Into Consideration That This Current Life Is
One Of Many Experiences In The Physical..."**
From VERONICA

47

Reincarnation

"We remember quite well the times of physical where the fear of physical death was of major concern. One identifies with the body, and its demise shifts the perspective of those immediately facing it.

Of course all eventually participate, it is the way of things.

However the design of life is to provide for many experiences, which is the base of the soul. Learning intense lessons is the opportunity for the soul energy to evolve.

There is satisfaction within when in between lives the soul energy has the ability to see the larger picture, that being the contemplation of all the lives and the progress made.

Your cultures in this time frame have created many belief systems to explain life. Most are incomplete devised to satisfy the focus of a singular life.

We are currently in the energy state. The lives we have lived are within our intellect's eye. The sum of the experience has expanded our energy.

From this view, the idea of just a single life opportunity would be disappointing, for the sum of one life would not have allowed for our total evolution.

To be in sync with our energy, all of the experience was necessary for balance and conclusion: Information always the height of our endeavor.

So we say to you reincarnation is a beautiful tool for energy to become more. It is a factual statement coming from one who is no longer physical.

It was an extreme blessing to participate in such a variety of moments so that we could share with you.

When your physical body dies your energy continues. There is complete recall of moments. Some so pristine and special that the idea of losing them is unbearable. Indeed there are difficult moments as well but in retrospect the best evolution was provided by them. That balance makes all experience something to be valued.

You have many opportunities for balance, appreciate them. Take in the lessons positive and negative. In the in between the value of them will be dear to you.

Live your life whether it is easy or not. Remember that there will be a moment where all of it will be of value."

-VERONICA

"There are people all the time who defeat the odds.
It is because they *choose* to..."
From VERONICA

48

Choices

"We have asked "how to do it" by many, who wish to resolve certain issues in their physical lives. Most aspire to view the obstacles that they perceive as external. The drama always the enemy needing to be overcome or extinguished.

In most of your region's cultures it is taught to always place description outside the self. Reality therefore becoming a villain that one has to deal with or place even farther outside of the self.

The energy perceived as God for most is a benevolent one who however sends difficulties necessary to evolve or become more holy. We would say to them that the "crosses to bear" issues to deal with or just plain difficulties are created by the self.

They are not sent by an outside source, they are created within you.

We realize the first reaction to such a response will perhaps be somewhat negative. For who would intentionally create suffering for themselves?

Certainly it is a test by God or some other outside force.

The responsibility for your reality resides within you. For every suffering there is a thought process creating the moment.

Great growth can accompany such creations if one is prepared to "own" the creations.

Contemplate carefully the choices presented by the eternal self. Connect if possible to the long term linear effects upon this current life and the moments beyond it.

Choices are the basis for evolvement while linear. Good or bad by your perception they have brought you to where you are right now.

If you are reading this narrative, then you are seeking a connection not a disconnection.

Give yourself credit for that.

Regard the choices as opportunities."

-VERONICA

49

Fear & Loathing in the Physical Realm

"To become part of the physical experience it is necessary to focus intensely upon the moment. A time line unfolds before you as you proceed upon creating a reality. The plans are in place but often a deviation occurs placing the energy in the path of alienation from the core energy from which they came. This occurrence is easily magnified and embellished by dramatic creations.

It is important to take notice of the embracement of drama and its ability to spiral into more complicated predicaments. It is at that point where the dread of continuance can cause severe depression and immobility. This overwhelming experience puts the souls of many in jeopardy due to the lack of movement in their energy.

To remedy this moment it is necessary to pause in the linear creation your are experiencing. Attempt to stop the unnecessary chatter in your head while focusing on a quite moment connection with your energy.

If it appears impossible, it is imperative to provide for yourself the silence. If you have the time to be miserable indeed you have the time to reconnect to your soul.

It's your choice. However, to continue in the turmoil will only result in more of what you find yourself in now.

Take the opportunity..... find the silence. It's quite alright to do it your own way. Just do it.

It's never going to be too late but the tardiness of your evolution will be noticed.... by you.

It is not required to be dissatisfied with your evolvement. It is not required to fear the moment. Fear can be conquered with mere eye to eye engagement. Fear will slink away by a mere glance of your internal energy. Yes it will.

Find the silent moment void of fear. Your distaste for the physical will recede and your eternal energy will emerge. Remember to keep linear chatter at bay. See what occurs."

-VERONICA

50

Seeing the Whole Soul: Not Just the Current Linear Manifestation

"In a difficult environment linear beings often become very disillusioned with the others around them. Some appear out right evil, some retain negativity in a peripheral way, while some cling to goodness while being sucked into an oblivion created by a psychotic mass consciousness.

What is a soul to do with that type of environment? Is all lost, or is there a formula to supersede the current linear in regard to soul intention?

We say yes there is.

It is important when dealing one-on-one to take into consideration the eternal aspect as well as the current linear. Often the physical presents only a limited perception of the individual involved. Or the individual is muddled into a vortex of many energies that do not define them at all.

What we are saying here is that it is relevant to look into the eyes of the soul rather than the eyes of the physical individual. Although the individual eyes are the windows we beseech a consideration of the soul rather than the physical form.

Often in your culture one makes an opinion of another based upon the actions or reactions in a singular linear life when actually it may be a collaboration of many lives.

Your religions preach of one life while the basis of the soul exists upon many. This leads to an inaccurate assessment of the energy involved.

Basically know the soul. Seek that energy alignment not just the current linear.

Multiple lives are a fact, therefore all must be considered when dealing with another. Not an easy concept but one we shall endeavor to present in your future moments."

-VERONICA

51

Loved Ones Lost

"We have spoken of this many times previously in this [book], however, repetition is sometimes warranted.

Death is a deceptive process when one is engaged in the linear especially if you perceive yourself left behind in the moment.

Everyone, including yourself is a physical manifestation of energy. The form you inhabit is an artistically chiseled performance of all your experiences and core energy personifications. When the physical dies all of those attributes continue eternally in the energy resulting from those experiences.

Your soul is an experience continuance regardless if it chooses to reincarnate or not.

If you find yourself "left behind" it is important to find clarity by understanding that your connection with the perceived person "lost" may continue.

Opportunities abound for conversations and energy blending if one can get past the sorrow at the loss of physical interaction.

Beyond this current moment there are many opportunities to connect. All one requires is the energy to do so. Nothing is ever lost.

The continuance is real.

Open your thoughts and your heart.

Those perceived as lost will find you, and continue the relationship."

-VERONICA

**"Your purpose universally is to evolve
and be more than before..."**
From VERONICA

52

To Those Who Have Read 52 Weeks of Messages From VERONICA and Others....
April Crawford Reveals Her Thoughts On This Process

"After a full year of [your] communicating with VERONICA, I thought it was time that the channel had a moment to speak.

I have been channeling many energies the past twenty years. It wasn't something I thought I'd be doing but here I am.

Throughout the past year, many of you have written really nice notes about your experiences with VERONICA that have made me feel like it's all worth it. For those who feel like I'm a fraud or on an ego trip, I wish you all could be in my shoes to have this experience.

It was wasn't my intention to be a channel but the relationship with spirit has certainly changed my perspective about everything.

I was raised a Catholic but always felt it a bit lacking in content. As an adult I sort of abandoned religion, just cruising along without a lot of focus on my spirituality.

The first experiences with channeling came unexpectedly. Though I enjoyed the experience, it was not something I was going to share with the world.

It was only through my husband Allen who gave me the anchor in physical that gave me the courage to explore other realms extensively.

I don't retain most of the channeling moments. If someone were to ask me what was said during a session I would not be able to answer.

I never read the newsletters, but I have read pieces of the articles, wondering at the fact that my hand wrote this. To keep it all pure I attempt to stay out of it as much as possible. There is always a humbling moment when I read a line or two. "This came from my hand!?" is the usual thought.

When going in and out of trance it's quite interesting to feel the different types of energies as they take up residence. I have never feared the process and always wonder at how many different energies there are.

Allen has always spoken of my fearlessness but I would say it is more of a great curiosity of something so much larger than myself. It's actually very cool.

I have never had a negative experience [trance channeling]. Spirit has always been refreshing and positive. They have taught me so much for which I am so grateful.

When I'm channeling there are a multitude of experiences that give "linear April" great hope and exclamation. I do not fear anything due to their interaction with me. If I had one wish, it would be that everyone would be connected to a channeling experience.

Nonlinear is very cool! And to experience it while linear is even better!"

--April

* * *

6288861R0

Made in the USA
Lexington, KY
05 August 2010